JIM BURNS

God
Made
Your
Body

BETHANY HOUSE PUBLISHERS
Minneapolis, Minnesota

DEDICATED TO
Rod and Pam Emery
I am so deeply grateful.

SPECIAL THANKS TO OUR ADVISORY PANEL:

Jennifer Degler, PhD

Nicole Frye, MA, LPC

Sandi Hofer, MA

Karl Williams, MD

God Made Your Body
Copyright © 2009
Jim Burns

Cover design by Lookout Design, Inc.

Interior design by Melinda Schumacher.

Scripture quotations are taken from the International Children's Bible®. Copyright © 1986, 1988, 1999 by Thomas Nelson, Inc. Used by permission. All rights reserved.

Published by Bethany House Publishers
11400 Hampshire Avenue South
Bloomington, MN 55438

Bethany House Publishers is a division of
Baker Publishing Group, Grand Rapids, Michigan.

Printed in China.

ISBN 978-0-7642-0211-7

Library of Congress Cataloging-in-Publication Data is available for this title.

A Special Note to Parents

Studies show that when children receive values-centered sex education at home, they are less likely to become sexually promiscuous and more likely to have a healthy view of their bodies and relationships. With the media introducing sexual topics to children at such a young age, there is no better countermeasure than parents introducing the concepts in this book to their children.

This book is part of a series of developmentally appropriate books called PURE FOUNDATIONS. *God Made Your Body* is for children ages 3 to 5. At this age, it's important to introduce children to the foundational theme that God created their body and it is special. You begin laying out for them a healthy view of their body and the very basics of sexuality. As you read this book to them, you will be establishing the trust that they can come to you when they are older to talk about these issues. You want to be the one to introduce the beautiful way God creates our bodies and that He has a plan for families.

Obviously, a book of this length will not cover every subject. It is meant to help you and your child develop a loving, trusting relationship where dialogue is the best teacher. And you'll discover spontaneous teaching moments from TV or other avenues to continue reinforcing a healthy view of sexuality.

Thanks for laying a foundation of trust and honesty with your child. You are giving your child a gift that will serve him for a lifetime.

Jim Burns, PhD

God made boys and God made girls.
God made all shapes and sizes.
He created all colors and languages.

God made *you*.

God made some boys and girls
with itty-bitty noses.

Some He made with
big ears.

God gave boys and
girls different colored
eyes—green, blue,
hazel, brown, or gray!

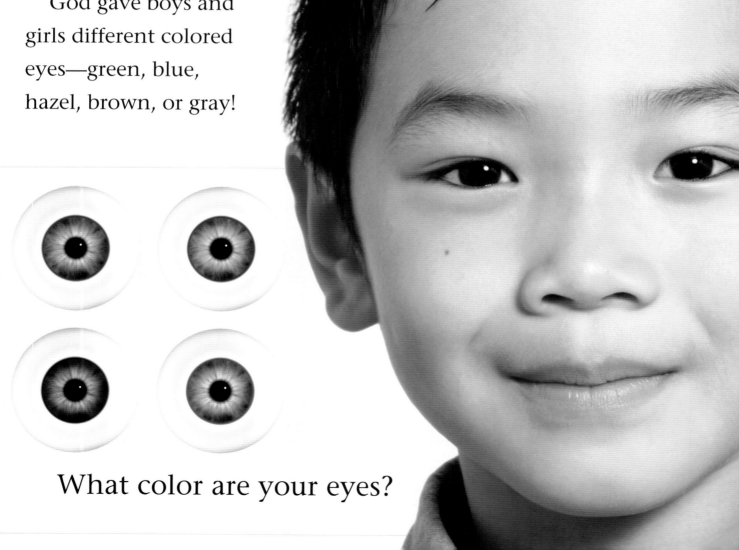

What color are your eyes?

Some boys and girls have skin dark like chocolate ice cream. Some have skin light like a vanilla milk shake. And most are in between.

God gave boys and girls different types of hair. Some hair is straight like a broom. Some hair is loopy like a crazy straw.

What kind of hair do you have?

God made some boys
and girls who like to tell
funny jokes.
He made some who like to sing or dance.
Some boys and girls can run fast like a
cheetah or kick a soccer ball far across a field.

8

Some boys and girls
make colorful pictures to put
on the fridge.

What are you good at doing?

In some ways, God made boys' bodies and girls' bodies alike.

He gave you eyes and ears and a mouth with teeth.

God made your toes to wiggle in the sand and your fingers to feel a puppy's soft ears.

He gave you a heart that keeps you alive and lungs to help you breathe.

What else did God give to both boys' bodies and girls' bodies?

In some ways, boys' bodies and girls' bodies are different. God gave boys special bodies, and He gave girls special bodies. What makes those bodies special?

Turn the page to find out!

penis

testicles

It was God's idea for every little
boy to have a penis and testicles.
Boys grow up to become men, and because
they have these special parts, they can
become daddies.

13

To every little girl God gave a vagina and a womb. Little girls grow up to become women, and because they have these special parts in their bodies, they can become mommies.

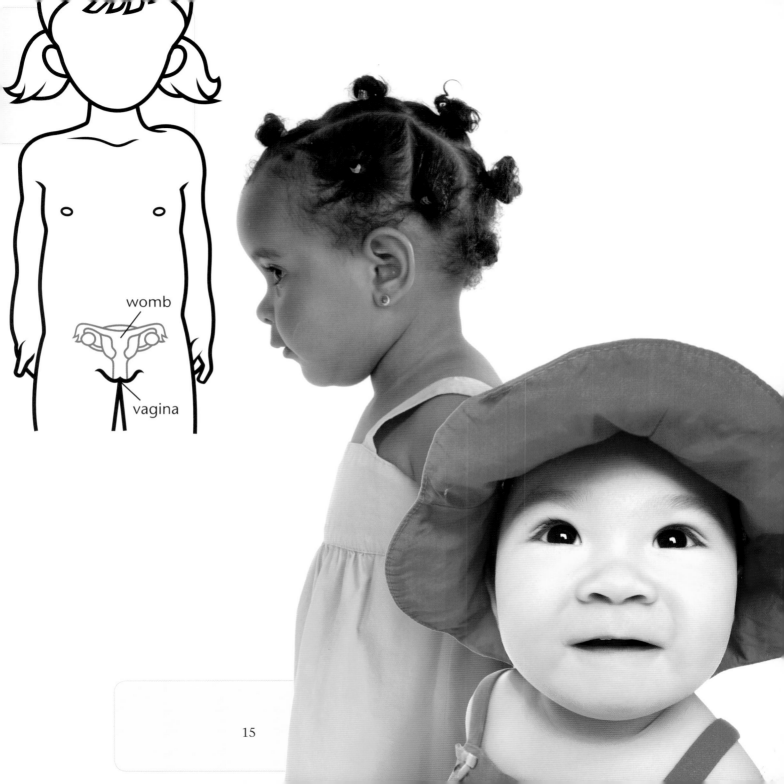

womb

vagina

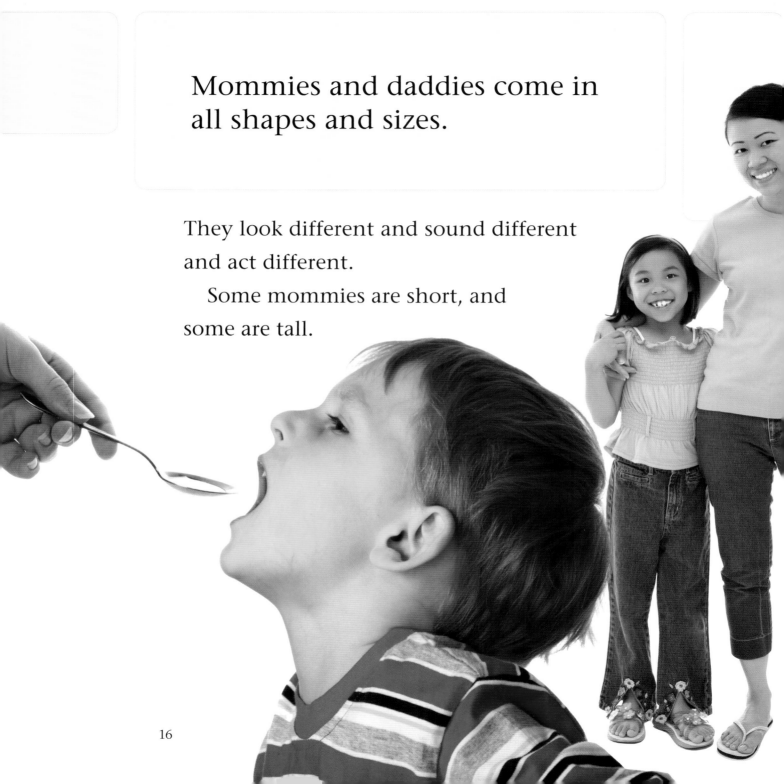

Mommies and daddies come in all shapes and sizes.

They look different and sound different and act different.

Some mommies are short, and some are tall.

16

Some daddies have bushy brown hair, and some have none at all!

Some mommies are good at fixing things or making an owie feel better.

Some daddies like to cook or ride a bike with you.

From a mommy and a daddy come children.

To make a baby, a mommy and a daddy come together in a special way called *making love*. Making love is something God made just for a husband and a wife to enjoy together.

When a mommy and daddy make a baby, they each give one special part of themselves. The daddy gives a part called a *sperm*. The mommy gives a part called an *egg*. The sperm and the egg join together inside the mommy to form an *embryo*.

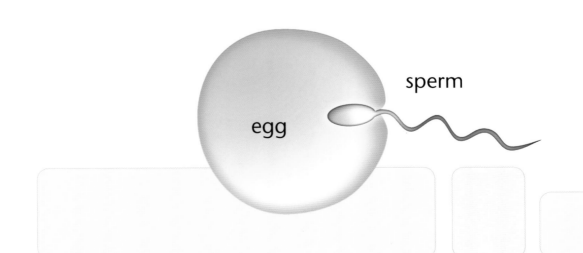

egg

sperm

All babies begin as an embryo in a mommy's womb, which is near her tummy. A baby grows and grows inside the mommy's womb. And the mommy's tummy grows and grows to make room for the baby.

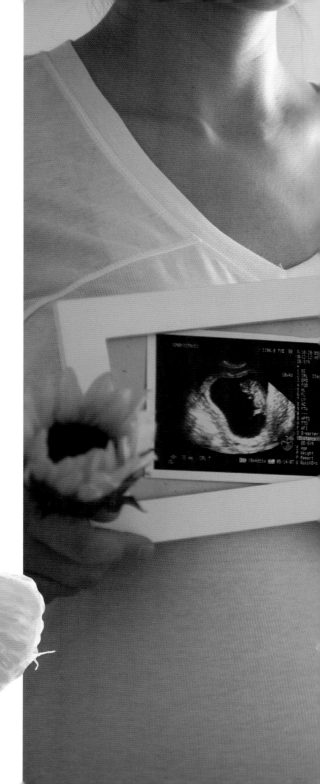

Here's how the baby grows in the womb:

One Month

The baby is already a boy or a girl. She has a heartbeat and is a little smaller than a Cheerio.

Three Months

The baby has hands and fingers and feet and toes. He can make a fist and stretch and kick. He might get the hiccups or suck his thumb and make faces. He's about the size of a large orange slice.

Six Months

The baby has grown so much! She now weighs about two pounds—as much as a bag of rice. She can hear sounds and sense light. She has sleep time and awake time, and her hair is starting to grow.

Nine Months

The baby is ready to be born! He is big enough and strong enough to live outside the womb now.

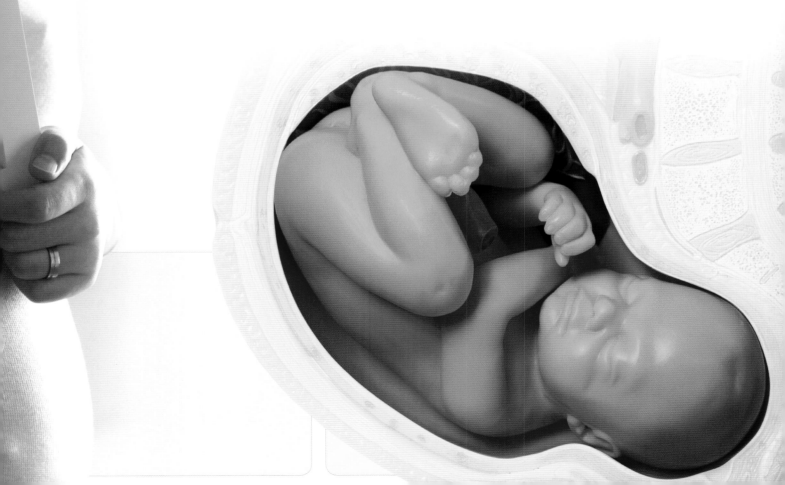

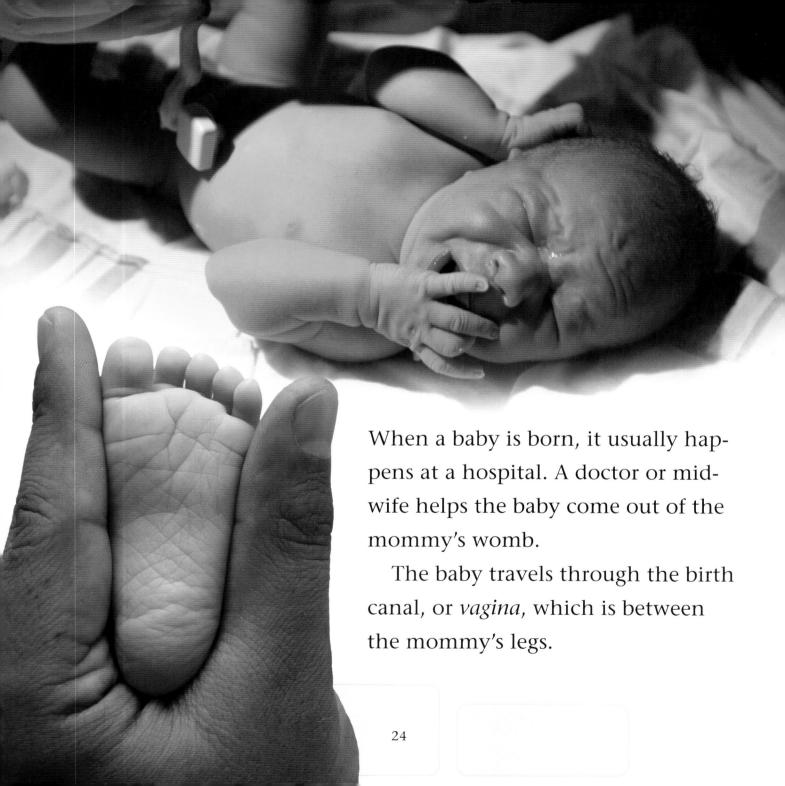

When a baby is born, it usually happens at a hospital. A doctor or midwife helps the baby come out of the mommy's womb.

The baby travels through the birth canal, or *vagina*, which is between the mommy's legs.

It is a very exciting and happy time! The baby's family has been waiting and planning for him for nine months! Already they love and care for him so much.

God loves you so much
that he put you
in a family.

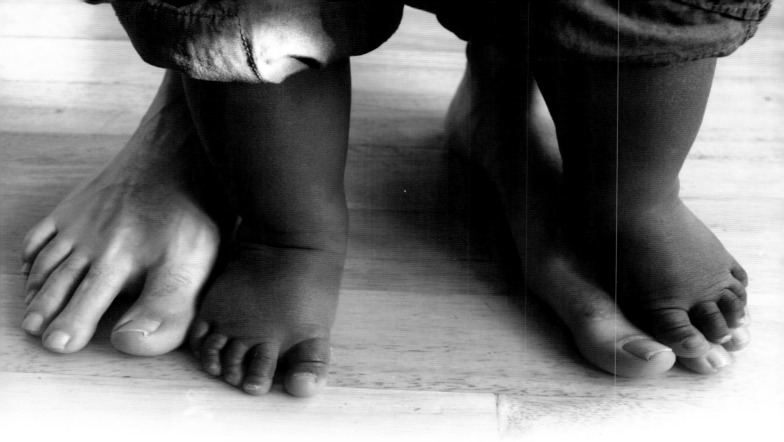

Most of the time, babies are born into their families.

Sometimes, babies are adopted into their families. Adoption happens when a child can't stay with his birth mother or father. The birth parents lovingly choose to have someone else raise the child. Another family wants to love the baby as their own, so he becomes part of that family.

No matter how you came to your family, you are God's special gift to them!

All families love each other and take care of each other. But every family looks different. Sometimes moms take care of us, and sometimes dads take care of us. Maybe you have a grandpa who sings silly songs with you. Or an aunt who takes you to the park. Maybe there are lots of children in your family. Or maybe it's just you!

What does your family look like?

Families are special.

Little boys and little girls
are special. *You* are special.
   God created you just as
He wanted you to be!

   Thank you, God, for
making boys and girls and
mommies and daddies.
   Thank you for
making my body.

Thank you for making **ME!**

You made my whole being.
You formed me in my mother's body.
I praise you because you made me
in an amazing and wonderful way.
What you have done is wonderful.
I know this very well.
You saw my bones being formed
as I took shape in my mother's body.
When I was put together there,
you saw my body as it was formed.
All the days planned for me were written
in your book before I was one day old.

PSALM 139:13–16 (ICB)